Centripetal Love

Centripetal Love

Dipendra Tamang

Copyright © 2024 Dipendra Tamang

Cover design and illustrations by Sharon Lim Sautarel

All rights reserved.

ISBN: 978-0-6483815-6-3

DEDICATION

To all those who are trying to find themselves.

CONTENTS

	Acknowledgments	i
	Definitions	iii
1	Breaking	1
2	Realizing	29
3	Finding	57

ACKNOWLEDGMENTS

I am profoundly grateful to my beloved wife Leena, whose unwavering support and boundless love have been my guiding light throughout this poetic journey.

Thankful to my parents for instilling in me a deep appreciation for language and the arts from an early age.

centripetal, adj
sen-ˈtri-pə-tᵊl

: proceeding or acting in a direction toward a centre or axis

love, noun
/lʌv/
: an intense feeling of deep affection

centripetal love
: a feeling of deep affection directed within yourself

1. BREAKING

Dipendra Tamang

Whisper

I whispered
"Who then will listen to my cries,
who then will heal my hurt?"
And a small voice within answered.
You.
You've always done it for yourself,
and this is no different.

Finding yourself can sometimes mean healing yourself.

Strong

I have suffered
but am not broken.
The hairline fractures
are a web that
makes me stronger.

Strong

Goodbye

Today I let go of you,
no angst or anger,
just sweet memories.
And a heart that knows,
it's for the best.

I don't let go easily,
but when I do,
there's no coming back.

Solitude

Don't mistake
my love of
solitude for loneliness,
I prefer the hum
of my thoughts
over the din of
meaningless conversations.

I'd rather be alone
than bored listening
to useless chatter.

Survive

Some days,
it's enough
to survive.
You can
always thrive,
when you are
back up again.

Survive

Fire

Don't play with fire,
they always told me,
but the fire within me,
they never did see.

Inner potential

Wildflower

I was never
one for the crowds
nor were the crowds
ever for me.
I have stood by myself,
got trampled upon
and ignored,
but that doesn't bother me.
For I stand alone,
proudly where I want to be.
I am the epitome
of a wildflower,
blooming alone
even when no one
is there to care.
For I follow
my own rhythm
and even the seasons
change for me,
not I for them.
I'm happy to be just here.

Wildflower

Embrace Life

To see the beauty in the flaw,
to feel love for the broken,
to appreciate the shortcomings,
is to come to terms with life
and that not everything is perfect.

To see beauty in the flaw,
to feel love for the broken,
is to embrace life.

Let Go

Sometimes,
your tendency
to romanticise the past,
holds you
hostage to growth.
Let go.
If it's over,
it's already over,
there's no sense
holding on to any of it.

Let go.

Endangered Species

I am an
emotionally
endangered species,
surviving
on indifference.
And I've learned
that apathy
can be a friend,
if you learn
how to befriend it.

Learning to become
your own best friend
is one of the best lessons ever.

Quiet

I know it's quiet,
that voice of yours,
right now.
But fret not,
the waters are
also calm
before the storm.
You will be heard again.

Quiet

Dipendra Tamang

Vagabond

I'm a vagabond soul,
studying life,
finding imperfection,
within and without,
and learning to live with it.

Acceptance

Scars

I have scars, on my body and in my heart. But I don't wear them proudly as many others do. Yes, I can understand the place they are coming from, that a battle was fought and maybe a war was won and that the scars are there to remind them of the hardship and victory they had to go through and still come out on top - alive and battle-hardened.

But I look at my scars and think, think of what I could have done differently so that there would not have been a battle at all. Couldn't I have been a bit more forgiving? A bit more understanding? A bit wider in the perspectives of things? Did I have to take it as an offence big enough for me to risk everything? And did I really gain anything out of winning the battle? Other than a few scars and untold graveyards of broken hearts left behind?

No, I'm not proud of my scars nor the story behind them. And it still pains me every time I look at them and I am reminded of other souls who carry the same scars, but just a little deeper than mine. Just because I'm good in a battle doesn't mean I have to bask in it, for that can become a habit and I'll be scarring others the whole of my life.

My scars are for introspection,
not for exhibition.

Level up

Yes,
the heartbreak
was real.
But so is
your healing.
Do not rush,
let it flow,
time needs
time to work.
You are now
levelling up.

Take your time, it's ok.

Tattoo

I tattooed over
the scars
you gave me,
but alas,
the needle couldn't
reach my soul.

Permanently marked but healing.

Value

I have always
valued your presence,
but it doesn't mean
that I will bend
over backwards,
just to accommodate your ego.

I value you,
but I respect myself more.

Letting go

Me letting go,
wasn't a mistake
or fear.
It was survival.

Holding on,
can sometimes mean the end of you,
so let go.

Wine

They trampled all over me
without realizing that
the sweetest of wines
are made that way.

*Don't be sad or give up
just because you are down,
it's a part of the refinement process.
Emerge stronger and sweeter.*

Pain

Pain is personal.
Pain is one of
those emotions
we don't
share easily,
because when we do,
we reveal
a part of our heart
and soul bare naked.
But when we finally do,
we can create magic,
because with the
one we love,
we love all their colours.

Love their all

Reminder

Pain is but a reflection
that you're alive,
letting you know
that you can still feel.
Reminding you of
your ability to heal.

Sometimes, bad things are a reminder
that good things are possible.

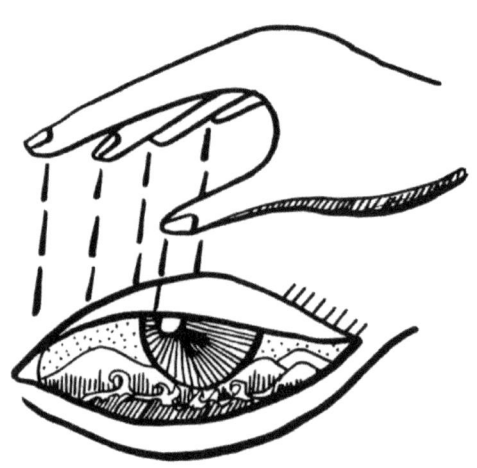

Stradivarius

To each of you
with a broken heart.
Remember,
even the best violins
were made only after
a tree was broken down,
do not worry,
you will sing again,
beautifully.

Remember, a tree had to be cut
to make a Stradivarius,
your melody will flow with time.

Bruised

Bruised hearts
feel the love,
more than others
will ever know,
for they have
lost it before.

*To know the pain
of a broken heart*

Resilience

Yes, I've been fractured,
broken down
and messed around.
Taken to the heights
and dropped down,
/
but
/
I've picked myself up,
put the pieces together again,
brushed away your dirt
and emerged stronger.
I may have lost a move,
but not the game,
and now, resilience
is my middle name.

Not staying down.

Signs

The ability
to acknowledge
that you are not okay
is actually a
sign of strength,
not of weakness.
Remember that.

Remember

Clouds

It's ok to fall,
for that's how
you learn to get back up.
And remember,
It's the rain that falls,
which gives life to all.

*Fall like the rain,
rise like the clouds.*

Dipendra Tamang

2. REALIZING

Dipendra Tamang

The Road

Love
is the road
we walk past
everyday,
no gates, no fences,
no guards,
yet we take
the other one
and wonder,
why love never
finds us.
If we only
took a minute
to look inside,
we would see
that the road
lies within us.

Search within and find your love

Breathe

Open all of the
windows that you had
shut and bolted.
Let the light
and warmth in,
so that you remember
what the sun feels like.
Don't be scared.
Just as thunderstorms
come but then pass,
so too will that pain.
Healing is just on the other side.

Breathe

Seven

I was seven
when I opened
the cage door
and
let the bird fly free.

After all these years,
I realize
I still have the love
and courage
to do it again.

Sometimes,
letting go
is more important
than holding on.

Unfollows

Sometimes
there are no
sweet goodbyes,
just
quiet
purposeful
unfollows.

*Letting go
in the times of
social media.*

Fall

If finding peace
means letting go
of pieces of your life,
then it's ok
to ruminate about
it and then do so.

Leaves fall,
and new branches grow,
breaking does not
necessarily mean
it's the end.
Sometimes
it's a means
to a new beginning.

Fall

Rainbow

All the colours
you hide within you,
would put a
rainbow to shame.
Open up and shine,
the world will be a better place.

Be a rainbow.

Worth

You are much more than someone else's opinion, their words, or their curses.

Yes, I know you have gone through a heartbreak, you have suffered, you have been let down, and felt like you could never get back up again. But you did, and now you have learned to love yourself, you have healed, put back those pieces together again. You are learning to trust yourself, and you finally have the courage to say, "I love myself." without feeling a shred of guilt. Yes, the nightmares of the past still haunt you, still makes you question yourself at times and most of all, makes you keep your guard up. You do not want to go through that again. This is understandable, no one wants to feel pain willingly.

But you are worth
much more than that.
You deserve much more.
You are much more than
someone else's opinion,
their words or their curses.
So let the guard down a bit,
not completely,
but enough for love,
if it should pass by, to filter in.

True strength

True strength
lies not in
mirroring the
shadows of those
who caused wounds
but in the
radiant resilience
of healing oneself
without adopting
the darkness that
once sought to define you.

Strength

Leaves

Some people
will fade out
of your life
by their own choosing,
there is no sense
in trying to
hold onto them,
new leaves grow
after every fall.
Let them go.

You'll be fine.

Aching Heart

I know it's messy and life has got you down. But remember that time, when your heart was so broken, and you thought nothing could be worse than the suffering of living? You came through in the end and found a depth within yourself that you hadn't known about. That's what pain and suffering do, it makes you dig deep within yourself and find strength you never realized that you had.

Pain is not to be idolized but rather accepted for what it is and then to be overcome. An aching foot or a scratched knee didn't stop you from learning to walk. So don't let an aching heart prevent you from learning to live, love and grow again.

Do not let an aching heart prevent you from
learning to live, love and grow again.

Self-discovery

The road to self-discovery
is not an easy one,
but the journey will be worth it.
You have to
confront your fears,
embrace your flaws
and forgive yourself
for past mistakes.
Through this process,
you will find
a love for yourself
that will be unbreakable,
and you will be
finally able to give
and receive love from
others in a healthier
and more fulfilling way.

Self-discovery

Bloom

With growth comes change,
one that may
not be understood
by those who dared not
bloom with you.

Let them be.

Acceptance

The first step
to healing is
embracing your emotions –
whether it be anger,
hurt, or confusion.
It's a vital part
of the process.
Feel them,
release them,
and pave your way forward.

Acceptance

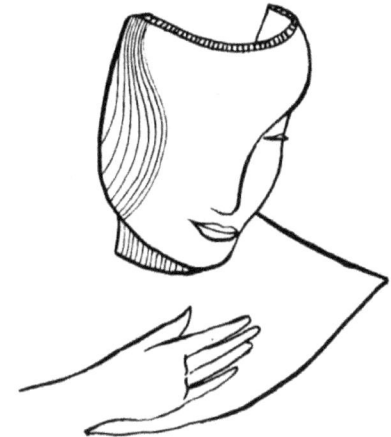

Journey

Perfection is a journey and not all of us complete it, but that doesn't mean we should be loved less for it.

I am fascinated with imperfections. With all of its flawed qualities and incomplete attributes. For therein lies the beauty of life and nature. It is learning to accept that not everything or everyone can be perfect and fully complete, that it is a process that takes time, a journey that not all of us will always complete, but that does not mean that we need to be loved any less or not accepted, or not tried to be understood.

We all have our values.
Remember, even a stunted tree still produces oxygen.

Transcend

In shadows deep,
where trust once lay,
A wounded heart
finds its own way.
With fragile steps,
it learns to mend,
To trust again,
to heal, to transcend.

A healing heart

Open

Let your healing
be from within
for that is where
your strength lies,
but be open
to help from
the outside too.
Like a flower
that blooms
by itself
but takes in
the water and the sun.

Open

Seasons

Sometimes you will not see what's right before your eyes, be it due to ignorance or the fact that you do not value it enough to grasp what it means to you. And in hindsight when you finally realize it's worth, the opportunity may be long gone due to the transgressions of time.

So, keep an open heart and an open mind, for opportunity, love, laughter, and smiles are always floating around us, it is just a matter of recognizing it and then accepting it to be a part of ourselves.

Take your time, but remember
that the seasons wait for none,
and the flowers will still bloom,
even without you.

River

When the time is right,
even the river will
change its course,
fret not,
your heart will find a way,
to let go of the pain.

*No matter how
dark and cold the winter,
spring will come
and flowers will bloom,
and you will heal.*

Non-linear healing

Healing
can be messy,
irregular
and chaotic
but that's okay.
A step backward
is a part of
growth and change.
You will move
forward again.
Always remember
that everyone heals
in their own way
and in their own time.

Healing is nonlinear

Growth

Today I want you
to remember that
suffering is not
an integral part of growth.
But yes,
growth after suffering
is possible.

It's not necessary to romanticize suffering and pain.

Moments

Remember to have
moments for your soul,
and with your soul,
for that is how you
discover the essence
of your authentic self.

Moments for yourself

Introspection

Healing takes time
and a bit of hurting,
and a whole lot more
introspection
than most people are
willing to do.

You heal as you realise

Updates

In the times of
constant status updates
and instant messaging,
I see you,
hurting in silence.

Alone.

Misunderstood.

Healing.

Take your time,
you don't have to
explain your life
to people who don't
have the capacity
for empathy and patience.

Metamorphosis
takes time but,
oh,
it will be so worth it.

This one is for those who don't share their hurt and are often misunderstood.
I see you; I feel you.

Final Growth

Sometimes in life,
you will go through
certain journeys
which will not feel
worth talking about
but then at the end
of it all,
you realize just
how essential it was
for your growth.

The journey wasn't beautiful,
neither was the destination.
But the growth at the end of it was worth it.

Authenticity

Authenticity
in what you do,
is an important aspect
of self-love and care.
Always remember that.

Be true to yourself

Dipendra Tamang

3. FINDING

Dipendra Tamang

Memories

How do you know you're healing?

When you remember them,
but those memories
do not haunt you, like they used to.

Healing

Within

If you think that love
is something given to you,
you're only partly right.
In truth,
love is something we create
within ourselves.
Hard times make you realize
that what you need
is mostly within you,
it is a matter of digging deep
and releasing it
and letting the love bloom.
Once you learn to trust yourself,
to believe in your own worth,
then your light will always shine.

The shine within.

Self-discovery

The path to self-discovery
can be challenging,
yet ultimately rewarding.
Along the way,
you will come to understand
that the love you yearn for
cannot be given to you by others;
it is a gift you need to give yourself.
Discovering a steadfast love
within yourself
illuminates a new perspective,
casting yourself in a brighter light.
This self-love
allows you to attract
positive and nurturing relationships
into your life.

Self-discovery

Crucible

In the
crucible of healing,
self-care
often languishes,
yet it is our
most vital ally.
Seek joy,
nourish,
and rest —
for in these,
true healing finds its place.

Where you find healing

Embrace

I used to believe
that love was something
only attainable from outside,
yet I was mistaken.
I have realized now
that a profound love
resided within myself.
I discovered the importance
of valuing my own solitude,
extending kindness to myself,
and persisting in
pursuit of my aspirations.
This self-love provided me
with the resilience
to confront any obstacle
and embrace life to its utmost.

It's all within.

Dipendra Tamang

Hope

Sometimes when your
days turn grey,
and darkness falls
and shadows loom,
do not wallow in
despair and gloom.
You have the strength
to light the way,
and bring back hope,
come what may.

Hope

Finding love within

I learned that to find love within myself, I needed to start by being kind and compassionate towards myself. This meant being gentle with my thoughts, forgiving of my mistakes, and embracing my flaws. That I needed to trust my intuition and never give up on myself.

It also meant that I needed to take care of myself, both physically and mentally. The process has helped me to understand that by taking care of myself, I proved that I was worthy of love and respect.

A crucial part of this journey has been surrounding myself with people who are positive and uplifting. I've learned to seek out relationships that bring happiness and fulfilment while avoiding toxic relationships that drain my energy and self-esteem.

This lesson has had a profound impact on my path towards self-love.

The path of self-love

Tears

Sometimes
pain may feel
overwhelming
and all hope
seem lost,
but remember
that in every tear
lies a seed of resilience,
waiting to bloom
and help you
rise back stronger than ever.

Tears

Self-love

Self-discovery is a crucial part of the journey towards self-love. Take the time to understand your values, goals, and dreams. Get to know yourself and your own strengths and weaknesses. Own your individuality and don't be afraid to be who you are.

Practice gratitude and mindfulness every day. Focusing on the present moment and finding joy in the simple things can help to cultivate a positive outlook on life. This will also help to keep one's mind focused on what they already have, rather than what they lack.

Set boundaries for yourself and learn to say "no" when necessary. It's important to prioritize your own well-being and to not allow others to take advantage of you. Practice self-care, doing things that make you feel good about yourself can help to boost your self-esteem and to cultivate a positive relationship with yourself. Be patient with yourself. Finding love within oneself is a journey, not a destination. It's important to be kind and gentle with yourself and to never give up.

The path of self-love.

Journey

The journey
towards self-love
may be challenging at times,
but it is also
incredibly rewarding.
Remember that
self-love is a lifelong journey.
No matter how much
you love yourself,
there will always be room
for growth and improvement.
Keep learning,
keep growing,
and never give up
on your journey towards self-love.
Embracing self-love
opens doors to fresh opportunities,
meaningful relationships,
and a life filled with
greater happiness and fulfilment.

A beautiful journey.

Trust

*Believe in yourself
and trust the one you love.
And if that one happens to be you,
trust yourself even more.*

This sounds simple but can be so very hard to do. Self-belief is one of the hardest things to do, especially if you have fallen, failed, or been superseded. The toils of time tend to bend even the strongest of wills. But we all know that what lies within us and what we are capable of, it is just that we refuse to see it at times, or it feels like the link has been broken and cannot be mended.

But if you look deep in your heart, you will find that ever since you were born, life has always been a challenge, nothing is easy, but we find fun in trying and learning. Why should that be any different when we mature and become adults? Take failure as a fall when you were learning to crawl, you didn't even think about the fact that you fell, just that it hurt, but you got back up again and tried it, again and again, till you mastered it. Take the same approach to any challenges you face in life, and you will come out on top. Or maybe at least learn that certain things are not for you, and you can try something else, like walking instead of crawling.

To trust the one you love, sounds fundamental. The very basic necessity of a sustainable relationship, but is life really that simple? There will always be moments of doubts, those little drips of water, seeping into the cracks of your heart, and then freezing up, thereby expanding, making the cracks wider each time. And if you have been hurt in the past, if you have felt that insurmountable pain, then you will know that each drop of that doubt will keep growing bigger. But you need to realize that you can't just ignore it and let it freeze and expand, we need to take it in, lubricate our cracks and make them easier to slide against each other. For the pain will never go away, the darkness will remain, but it is unto us, to make it work for us instead of against us.

It's a wonderful feedback loop.

Deserving

I hope
you realise
that you are
deserving of
kindness and care
and that
you don't have
to look far,
for it begins
with self-compassion
and self-love.

You are deserving.

Treat yourself well

I hope
you realize
that finding love
within oneself
means accepting
who you are,
flaws and all.
It means
understanding that
you are deserving
of love and
treating yourself
with the same kindness
and compassion
you would give to others.

Treat yourself well.

Validation

When you find
love within yourself,
you no longer need
validation from others
to feel good about yourself.
You become your own
source of validation
and know that you are
enough just as you are.

You are enough.

Dipendra Tamang

Embrace yourself

Learn to let go of the pain,
embrace yourself and let it flow,
For you will find within,
a love that sustains,
a light that continues to glow.

Glow within

Compass

Self-love
is the compass,
guiding us
through destiny's maze,
as we learn
that fate favours
those who embrace
life's unpredictable ways.

Self-love always points the right way.

Embrace

I searched for love in every place,
But found it only in my own embrace.
I hold myself and feel the love,
A gift from heaven up above.

Self-love

Self-love
let's you know
that you are enough
just as you are.

That you do not
need external validation
to accept yourself
and be happy with
who you are.

Self-love.

Resilient Heart

Deep within,
where courage lies,
A heart beats strong,
defying goodbyes.
Through trials faced,
it finds its way,
The resilient heart
leads the way.

Resilient heart

Lanterns of connections

I am walking my path
of self-discovery alone,
yet I cherish the
lanterns of connections
that illuminate the way forward.

Lanterns

Don't rush

Healing takes time
and patience
and it is important
to nurture and
give yourself the love
and care that you require.
Do not mistakenly
rush to fill the void
or settle for something
or someone less.
Allow yourself time
to rest and heal.

Take your time.

Metamorphosis

The old me is still here,
I don't run,
I don't hide.
I just evolve.
But remember,
the soul in the caterpillar
is the same as in the butterfly.

Metamorphosis

Inner light

Within you lies
a love so true,
A light that shines
in all you do.
And your journey of
self-love will begin,
Once you find it
deep within.

Inner light

Transformative healing

Through the transformative
process of healing,
scars evolve into
narratives of resilience,
and pain finally finds its purpose.

Transformative healing

Long route

The passage to receiving
what you deserve
may seem long,
but know that the
destination doesn't change
and sometimes
the longer route
is the better one in the end.

Deserving

Process of healing

Healing
is not something
that happens at once
or just once.
It is a process
that requires
patience, self-compassion
and belief.
You need to learn
to allow yourself
the time and space
to heal and trust
that the journey is worth it.

It takes time

Stronger Healing

You may cause the heartbreak,
but resilience is strange.
The harder the fall,
the stronger the heal.

I will heal,
I will walk,
and then I will bloom.

Vulnerability

It is ok to be vulnerable
about yourself at times
or about certain aspects
of yourself.
That is how you learn
to know yourself better,
thereby expanding yourself
and then emerging stronger and better.

Your vulnerability
is not a flaw
but rather a pathway
to know yourself better
and emerge stronger.

Self-discovery

The path to
self-discovery
is not an easy one,
but the journey
will be worth it.
You have to
confront your fears,
embrace your flaws
and forgive yourself
for past mistakes.
Through this process,
you will find
a love for yourself
that will be unbreakable,
and you will be finally
able to give and
receive love
from others in a healthier
and more fulfilling way.

Self-discovery

Show how you heal

I'm not asking you to stay with someone who breaks your heart, but instead to show them how you suffered and how you heal. Painful as the process may be, accidents do happen in life, and love is no different. Sometimes the best of intentions at the wrong moment can lead to an utterly heartbreaking moment. It is precisely at those times that you should realize that a broken heart doesn't necessarily mean a broken love.

Just as in life, setbacks make us stronger, let that be so in love as well. Heal the heart by letting go of the ego if the actions that led to it were unintentional. And if it was premeditated, what better way of showing your strength, character and light than by healing yourself and forgiving. You are the winner either way.

Find the one who breaks your heart
and show them how you heal.

Footsteps

The footsteps
you hear
are just echoes
Listen closely
and you'll see
that they are yours.
As you walk
away from the past
and into love.

The walk to self-love.

Healing

Healing is in letting go. It is the letting go of the emotions that hurt you, of the dark thoughts that keep you awake at night, of the constant questions that keep coming into your mind, even when you don't want it to.

Jealousy, envy, anger, and loathing, all come into play, and all must be dealt with. Not so easy to let them go, but if you open your heart to the context, the experience, and the need, you can do it. It will haunt you for a while, pain doesn't go away immediately, nor do relationships end abruptly.

Our brain may be a mass of electrical impulses, but there's no single switch to turn off feelings and emotions. It is a slow process, as each emotion, each feeling is allowed to feel itself to the fullest and then laid to rest.

Healing is in letting go.
Let each memory feel itself to the fullest
and then lay it to rest.

Stardust

You
are the
essence of a star,
so never forget
that there's
light within,
even in the darkest of hours.

We are all stardust.

Resilient

Resilience is a wonderful thing. Leave a box over a field of grass for a week and then move it away. You will notice that it's probably become yellow and almost dead, but let it be for a while and you will see in a few weeks' time, that it's green and growing again. That is the resilience of the grass.

But that is nothing compared to the resilience of the heart. Time and again, ever since we are babies, we break it, we abuse it, and we don't even think twice about it. We desire material things, physical connections, heart connections, and when we don't get them, we are distraught, but the heart carries on. We learn to live through disasters, the loss of a loved one, the heartbreak caused by the fallout from love. All of these breaks our heart, but it still beats on, resolute.

It may feel like we cannot carry on at times, but we trudge on and suddenly one day realize that we are looking at the world through different lenses again. For the heart knows not to give up. The heart is resilient, and the heart is much bigger than we think it is.

You broke my heart,
yet I forgave you.
It was then I realized,
how big and resilient,
my heart truly was.

Healing is

Healing is not in forgetting.
Healing is not in forgiving.
Healing is in letting go,
and learning to love yourself again.

You don't have to forget to heal,
and you don't have to forgive to heal,
but once you're healed, you'll probably do both

Melody

Even if you
feel empty inside,
don't give up on hope,
just as a hollow guitar
produces melodies
when in the right hands,
so will you,
with the right one.

Your time will come,
you will make music.

Right way

Loving someone right,
is not enough.
You have to love
yourself the right way too.

Self-love is essential

Self-sufficiency

Resilience
is built upon
self- sufficiency
and dependence
upon others
is not a garden
you want to grow in.

Self-sufficiency

Music

In a world that has forgotten to listen,
be like the birds that still sing their song.

Make music and carry on, live for yourself.

As I am

Love me as I am
or let me be,
for I'm finally
learning to love
all these sides of me.

All of me

Self-belief

I see you and the pain, doubt, and conflicting emotions within. I can see you are making a real effort, but the sliver of self-doubt continues to haunt you. Each day is a struggle and every decision feels like it is draining your soul.

Sanity has a new meaning as you try to redefine it. Anxiety has become second nature, and all support systems seems to be on wheels, ones that are moving away.

I know it is hard, it is difficult and feels hopeless at times, but remember, the real power lies with you. It is time to take the power back from the one who made you feel this way, who brought down your feeling of self-worth to this. It is time to believe in yourself.

The power of self-belief is beyond any explanation. And once you believe in yourself, you will find that others will truly begin to believe in you.

Once you believe in yourself,
you will find that others
will truly begin to believe in you.

Vibrant Soul

What is it that you are searching for,
when you have that faraway look in your eyes?
Is it the bittersweet truths of yesterday,
or the shock of camouflaged lies?
Has the chemistry of kiss gone amiss,
that your tongue feels like sandpaper.
Are you wishing to exhale it all,
the pent-up thoughts, words, and curses.
For the pain I see you go through,
is real, heart-rending, and palpable.
Look at the mirror, and see yourself without doubt,
not as they want you to be, but as you truly are -
A vibrant soul, an embodiment of beauty,
at peace with yourself, within and without.

Look at the mirror
and see yourself
without doubt,
as you truly are.

Mirror

The mirror
reveals a truth:
your worth
is immeasurable.
Believe in your
unique essence,
and embrace
the person you are.
And like autumn leaves,
doubts will fall away,
leaving you standing
tall and unyielding.

Embrace yourself

Dreams

When our dreams
seem distant,
and goals unsure,
Belief lets us know
that we have the power.
It grows in us
a sense of worth,
Unleashing our potential,
and a whole new rebirth.

Self-Belief

Don't give up

Challenges
are opportunities
for growth,
and you have
the power to
overcome obstacles.
Better things await
those who make
an effort and
keep trying.
Believe in yourself
and keep pushing forward.
The journey is worth it,
and the destination even more so.

Don't give up

North Star

Faith leads us
when we feel alone,
like the North Star
in a world unknown,
And with each step,
the doubts disappear,
as we trust ourselves
and persevere.

Trust and persevere

Blessings

Even though
it can be hard,
sometimes
you will realize
that your struggles
are a blessing in disguise,
for those experiences
can lead you to
the realization that
you are enough.
You learn to love
who you are,
and to never compromise
on your own
happiness and well-being.
This self-love
gives you the courage
to pursue your dreams
and to keep the company
of people who love
and support you.

Blessings in disguise.

True happiness

It is ok
to listen
to others
but do not
get caught up
in their opinions
and expectations,
because
true happiness
and fulfilment
comes from within.

True happiness

Shine

In every soul,
a universe dwells,
Echoes of stars,
where magic swells.
You're a tapestry of
galaxies near and far,
remember to shine,
like the star that you truly are.

Shine

Centripetal Love

Take some time, sit back, and think. Think of all the things you held on to - your thoughts, your beliefs, and your superstitions. Of all the people you held on to in the hopes that you would be counted as a better person. And all the material things you thought important - for your leisure, pleasure, or desire.

Now think back of the times when that didn't count. When your beliefs didn't stand the test of time or reason. When your superstition was just that, a poor lonely cat crossing the street or perhaps going back home. The times you were let down by the ones you hoped were your friends, even though deep down you knew, knew that it was superficial. But hope is a tragic thing. It keeps us running.

But you see now, don't you? You made it past all those disappointments, those rejections, those falls. You really didn't need them. The strength was always within you. It is just difficult to see in salty waters. Now go dry those tears up because hope is a wonderful thing. It keeps us running. And that's the thing with hope, it keeps us positive. Always looking, expecting, and wondering. Looking outwards to the world and also looking inwards, within ourselves. And that's why I call it Centripetal Love. An alchemy of love, hope and desire, which not only searches outside but digs deep within. And always finds the strength, the hope, the belief within ourselves.

Let go,
You deserve it.

Inner Strength

When life gets tough,
don't lose your way,
believe in yourself,
don't let it sway.
You hold the strength
to rise above,
and conquer all
with courage and love.
Believe in yourself
and you will find,
the power to leave
all the troubles behind.

Inner strength

Love yourself first

Have you ever
been so hurt
or broken
that you just went
back to your shell?
Only to realize later,
that at the end
of it all,
you matter most
to yourself.
That you deserve
to give all the love
to yourself first.

And I never went back to anyone,
I just went back to myself,
for I understood that I deserved me
better than anyone else.

Quiet

I know it's quiet,
that voice of yours,
right now.
But fret not,
the waters are
also calm
before the storm.
You will be heard again.

Quiet

Firefly

A firefly glows in the dark,
not for you or me, but for itself.
Be like that firefly,
and glow from within, for yourself.
Too many claim the moon anyways

*Do you need to remind someone
that they have the glow within?*

Rain

Learn to love
like the rain,
without a care.
The rain
doesn't care
if it falls on a
parched land
or the lake,
it gives all it has
for it knows that it
will soon be back again.
Pour out your love
in the same way,
for in the end
it will all flow back to you.

Love like the rain.

Constellation

I come
with my
own storms,
but
within me
lies a universe of love.
Embrace both,
and you'll find
a constellation of
strength in my heart.

Constellation

Within

When you have
gone through a
storm of emotions
and hardships,
you realize that
the key to happiness
is not in finding love
outside of yourself,
but within.
You learn to cherish
your own company
and find peace
in solitude.
You discover that
loving yourself
is the foundation
for all other
forms of love
in your life.

It's always within you.

Centripetal Love

www.ingramcontent.com/pod-product-compliance
Lightning Source LLC
Chambersburg PA
CBHW062051290426
44109CB00027B/2788